Buy the Dip?

Investing in Decentralized Finance and Trading Cryptocurrency, 2022-2023 - Bull or bear? (Smart & profitable strategies for beginners)

Bit Bros Media

Disclaimer

Stocks, bonds, crypto, everything goes down: now what?

For investors, it has been a bad year so far. On both stocks, and bonds and cryptos you lost a lot of money this year and with money in the bank you also lose, because the inflation rate in April was almost 10 percent. Where can you still go with your money if you do want to make some money?

For years, low interest rates were investors' best friend. Because bank savings yielded hardly anything due to the low interest rates, much more money went into equities. And that drove up the prices considerably, which in turn brought investors a lot of return.

For example, last year you earned 28 percent with the AEX index, the leading index of the Amsterdam stock exchange. But this year the AEX index already fell by about 15 percent. Only four of the 25 AEX funds are in profit.

Bonds then? If interest rates fall, as they have in recent years, that will be good for bond prices. There will be a lot of demand for existing bonds, because their interest is usually higher than the market rate. If that starts to rise again, that advantage will be gone. And the prices of bonds will fall. On Dutch government bonds, you already lost 10 percent this year.

Afraid of higher interest rates

2

The reason that stocks and bonds are doing badly is that investors are afraid that the current high inflation in the eurozone and the U.S. will lead to central banks raising interest rates. Central banks traditionally try to combat too high inflation with higher interest rates.

The U.S. has already started to do so and analysts think that interest rates will be raised further there. Christine Lagarde, ceo of the ECB (European Central Bank), has said that a start will be made on raising official interest rates in July.

Cryptos then?
There is nothing to be gained from crypto currencies this year either. The price of bitcoin, by far the most important crypto, is now about 40 percent lower than at the beginning of the year.

Bitcoin was sold as the digital gold, but with bitcoin you don't get compensation such as interest or a share of the profits, says Stan Westerterp, owner of Bond Capital Partners. "With interest rates rising, bitcoin is becoming less attractive."

Cash?
Should you have left your money in the bank then? Mwah, the interest rate is zero, and if you have more than a ton in the bank you even pay 0.5 percent interest. Worse, your money will be worth less anyway due to inflation.

According to our own CBS (Central Bureau of Statistics), a euro was worth 9.6 percent less in April than a year earlier.

Gold and homes

There are, however, investment categories where prices did rise. In April, for example, homes were on average 13.7 percent more expensive than one year earlier. But buying a house as an investment is not for everyone.

The price of gold also rose, by almost 1 percent. After the Russian invasion of Ukraine, gold was seen as a refuge in these uncertain times. And investors also often step into gold when inflation is rising.

Energy stocks

So is there nothing left that you can invest in? The only investment that is doing well at the moment is energy equities, says Jacob Schoenmaker. In the AEX, for example, Shell is by far the strongest riser this year, with a gain of more than 37 percent.

"But you shouldn't put all your money into energy companies, because if sentiment turns, those prices will probably fall again."

Or insurers

It is possible that banks and insurers can still benefit from higher interest rates, Schoenmaker thinks. For them, unlike equities in general, higher interest rates are actually beneficial. But if share prices fall, insurance companies in particular will suffer, Schoenmaker says.

It is important, however, to spread your investments, Schoenmaker warns. So don't put all your eggs in one basket. That means you can't avoid putting part of your money into investments that are currently being hit hard.

Table of Contents

The market in early 2022

More and more independent entrepreneurs are making the decision to invest in cryptocurrency and stocks. For example, since the beginning of the pandemic, the bitcoin price has been more than interesting for people who want to take a leap into the deep end of the crypto world.

Investments in other crypto currencies are also increasing. Think of the XRP of ripple or the Ether of Ethereum. Are you also planning to start with digital money as a self-employed entrepreneur? In this article, you can read more about what you need to know about investing in cryptocurrency in 2022.

Know how crypto works before you start investing First, it's good to know how crypto works before you spend money on it. Recent research by Radar shows that the majority of crypto owners have no idea how crypto exactly works. The fact is that there are different types of virtual coins that you can invest in. The most well-known is bitcoin, which is also the very first crypto currency. In 2009, the first transaction with bitcoin was sent by founder Satoshi Nakamoto. A year later, in 2010, the first commercial transaction took place. Two pizzas were purchased for 10,000 bitcoin.

With the knowledge that one bitcoin is worth over $ 34000 at the time of writing, you can hardly imagine. Over the years, bitcoin has become incredibly valuable. More and more people have started to invest in it and the blockchain, on which the currency operates, has become increasingly stronger and more secure. In addition to bitcoin, there are other crypto currencies you can invest in. Take for example the XRP on the ripple exchange rate or the Ether or the Ethereum exchange rate. These altcoins are worth slightly less than bitcoin, but certainly not less interesting. So look carefully which coins fit into your portfolio.

Are you going to invest in crypto for business or private use?
Once you've delved a little into the ins and outs of cryptocurrencies, it's good to look at how you're going to invest in one or more coins. After all, as an entrepreneur, you can take the gamble both in business and in private. You should know that when you decide to go into cryptocurrency for business purposes, any profit or loss will be included in your company's total profit. Thus, in doing so, your possession in crypto is considered as the possession of your business. You must therefore always report the results of your investment in, for example, the bitcoin exchange rate on the profit and loss account.

Of course, this affects your administration as a self-employed person. Therefore, it is always recommended to hire an accountant when you want to invest in crypto for business purposes. Because business investment is seen by many entrepreneurs as a kind of burden, they often choose to invest money privately. In that case you don't have to include any loss or profit in your total turnover and profit. What you do have to take into account is the tax authorities. Investments made privately are always taxed in Box 3 with a capital gains tax of 0.6% to 1.6%. You must therefore determine yourself, or in consultation with your accountant, which way of investing suits you best.

Does the situation in Russia and Ukraine affect crypto?
So far, 2022 has been an eventful year, just like 2021 and 2020. It is not surprising if you, as an entrepreneur, are wondering if you should invest at all in the bitcoin rate, ripple rate or any other rate. The last few years have been very rosy for the various cryptocurrencies. Corona played a big role in the sudden rise on the prices: first, big investors, companies and entrepreneurs started investing in crypto when the economy collapsed. As a result, the prices suddenly went up, which in turn attracted the interest of "ordinary" people and self-employed people. You guessed it: they too decided to start investing in crypto en masse.

So the corona crisis did a lot of good for crypto currencies. Now that this crisis seems to be coming to an end, the next one is already on the horizon: the possible war in Ukraine. If you currently own crypto currencies, chances are you've already seen the prices drop a bit in recent weeks. Experts expect the bitcoin price to drop even further in the event of an actual war. The prices of other altcoins also took a hit in the last two weeks. Does that mean you shouldn't invest in crypto at all? Certainly not. You should, as usual, only invest with money that you can possibly spare. Then the bitcoin price or the ripple price is an incredibly fun and exciting adventure to follow.

What is Bitcointrading?

Simply put, Bitcointrading involves exchanging fiat money for this crypto currency. Digital platforms like Bitcoins Era allow people to buy Bitcoin with conventional money and sell it later. This allows you to research and predict the Bitcoin price to determine when to buy or sell it for profit. You may be able to sign up on this platform to begin trading Bitcoin.

Financial firms have Bitcoin-based investment products, including contracts for difference, in addition to crypto exchanges. Such products allow you to trade Bitcoin without owning It directly. Overall, Bitcoin trading is a developing activity that people are practicing to make a profit. Here's why you should start trading Bitcoin this year as well.

Valuation of Bitcoin

Most of the factors that affect the value of fiat money, such as government debt, interest rates and political instability, do not affect the price of Bitcoin. While this crypto currency fluctuates rapidly, its value rises gradually. Moreover, the demand for Bitcoin is high due to its increasing acceptance and application. Moreover, blockchain technology regulates the supply of Bitcoin, not governments and central banks.

Today, miners are producing new tokens, and people are trading these crypto coins for profit. Some investors have achieved more than 100% returns on their Bitcoin investments. Moreover, Bitcoin reached a record value of more than $60,000 per token. Such details should encourage you to start trading this virtual currency today.

Some economists have predicted that the value of Bitcoin will eventually reach the $1 million mark. That's because countries like El Salvador have made Bitcoin a legal tender and more businesses are now accepting it as a means of payment.

Some are afraid of Bitcoin because banks and governments could control its value, but others are joining in. And as more central banks buy Bitcoin as their currency reserve, its value will skyrocket, making Bitcoin owners richer.

Bitcoin is secure.

Bitcoin uses blockchain technology to secure transactions. You may want to start trading this virtual currency today, as it uses a peer-to-peer network to allow for anonymous exchanges. Ideally, you are not disclosing any personal information when you sell services and items or pay with Bitcoin.

The transaction does not reveal your real identity when you sell or buy Bitcoin. In addition, Bitcoin transactions are cheaper and almost instantaneous. No one outside

the trade has access to details such as the parties
involved and the amounts. In addition, the Bitcoin
blockchain prevents crypto-currency counterfeiting and
double-spending...

Luna (Terra) has been shut down?

There are again some major developments to report regarding Terra (LUNA), the cryptocurrency that has completely collapsed. For example, some exchanges have pulled the altcoin from their platform and the network has paused.

Terra pulls the plug on blockchain
Early this morning it was reported that Terra has frozen its blockchain. This is the second time this has happened in the past day. The network's validators pulled the plug on the blockchain at block level 7,607,789 with the goal of developing a plan for how to proceed.

As a result, no crypto can be sent over the network anymore. For how long this will be the case is unclear. However, it is an annoying scenario for people who currently still have LUNA. After all, they have no way to go.

Crypto trading platform pauses LUNA trading
The Dutch trading platform Bitvavo has decided to pause trading in LUNA. Because the network is completely down, there is little liquidity. It also means that users cannot currently withdraw LUNA from their Bitvavo account.

However, the exchange is coming up with a compensation plan as the current situation means that users with LUNA in their account may have "unwanted exposure" to the cryptocurrency. The compensation consists of the following:

"Users will receive the EUR value of their LUNA at the time the LUNA-EUR trade was paused 13-05-2022 8:20 AM (CET). These amounts will be automatically added to the user account later today (while the user keeps their LUNA) and will be visible in the transaction history."

So users get to keep their LUNA and can withdraw it once the blockchain is up and running again. But as mentioned, it is not clear when this will be and if it will happen at all.

Binance removes LUNA completely
Crypto exchange Binance is going a step further and removing the LUNA and UST trading pairs from its trading platform. The exchange announced this early this morning.

The truth about Terra

The price of terra (LUNA) has fallen a whopping 99% in recent days to $0.05, its lowest price since the end of 2020. LUNA was still in the fifth spot in terms of largest cryptocurrencies last week, but is falling to position 128 at the time of writing. The UST stablecoin that caused this situation is currently 60% below its value.

Still, the creators of Terra don't want to give up and are coming up with a rescue plan for LUNA as well as for UST. Terra founder Do Kwon, CEO of Terraform Labs, unveiled the first measure yesterday.

With community proposal 1164, the team wants to save UST by increasing the base pool. The amount of UST that can be exchanged for LUNA will then be quadrupled. This will ensure that UST owners can still cash out, but will also put even more pressure on the LUNA price. The proposal has now received 62.6% of the votes in favor.

New measures for LUNA & UST
Recently, Terraform Labs revealed even more measures to save this crypto. First, the team wants to destroy the remaining UST tokens in Terra's community pool. This will involve a whopping 1 billion worth of UST being destroyed in this token burn. Normally this pot would be worth $1 billion, but at the time of writing it is only $400 million.

In addition, the team is going to retrieve 371 million UST stored (wrapped) on Ethereum (ETH) back to Terra for subsequent destruction as well. That means a total of almost 1.4 billion UST will be destroyed, about 11% of the total supply.

Finally, TerraForm Labs is going to tie up 240 million LUNA tokens to protect the Terra network. Because the exchange rate has plummeted so much, the chances increase that someone can buy a huge amount of LUNA to carry out a so-called 51% attack. This person could then temporarily take over the network, but the strapped LUNA should prevent that.

There is a very skeptical response to the proposals, but then the fear is well established. In fact, the panic is so great that other stablecoins are currently becoming slightly unstable. For example, people are selling USDT in exchange for USDC.

SEC investigating Terra?

It is not inconceivable that the U.S. Securities & Exchange Commission (SEC) is not happy about the saga surrounding Terra (LUNA) and the stablecoin UST. In fact, two former lawyers at the SEC have reported to The Block Research that the SEC has most likely already launched an investigation into Terraform Labs in the meantime.

SEC Investigates LUNA

Philip Moutakis, a former lawyer at the US regulatory agency, revealed today that he assumes the SEC has already started an investigation into Terraform Labs. According to him, it is obvious that the SEC has not been idle in the past few days, especially since the SEC already started an investigation into Mirror Protocol.

Terraform Labs' founder, Do Kwon, was also the man behind this Mirror Protocol.

"The SEC is already on the ground, they are investigating Mirror Protocol," Kwon said.

However, a spokesman for the SEC declined to comment on a possible investigation into Terraform Labs and UST. According to him, the SEC cannot say whether an investigation is underway, but they are also unable to say that it is not. Unclear, in other words.

Stablecoin regulation

Stablecoins have long been a thorn in the side of regulators around the world and the SEC is no different. Last year, the chairman of the SEC, Gary Gensler, called stablecoins "poker chips." A regulatory framework for stablecoins has been in the works for some time and perhaps the demise of UST will accelerate the process.

Do Kwon, on April 21 of this year, commented on the fact that according to the SEC stablecoins could possibly be seen as securities. According to him, this notion is utter nonsense. Philip Moutakis, however, argues that it is not that simple:

"Even if there is a question of whether UST is a security," Moustakis continued, "Even if the stablecoin,as designed, may have escaped the application of the federal securities laws, subsequent transactions may bring the stablecoin back under the jurisdiction of the SEC."

Stablecoin troubles?

The past few days have been dominated by the complete collapse of Terra (LUNA) and its associated stablecoin UST. UST lost the peg with the US dollar and as a result the price of LUNA collapsed by more than 99%. Immediately, people began to worry about other stablecoins. To the shock of many crypto investors, the value of Tether (USDT) was also below $1 today.

Tether below $1
The collapse of LUNA and UST had a major impact on the crypto market. Yesterday was a fire-red day and most cryptocurrencies fell by double digits. Even bitcoin (BTC) did not manage to hold on and dropped below $29,000. A similar debacle for by far the largest stablecoin, Tether, could throw quite a bit of oil on the fire.

At the time of writing, Tether is trading on most major exchanges, such as Binance, for less than $1. While crypto investors are obviously not waiting for this after yesterday, it is too early to say that anything is really going on. In fact, Tether is now trading for around $0.98, with a bottom of $0.956 on FTX. That's not $1, of course, but it cannot yet be said that Tether has substantially lost the peg with the U.S. dollar.

"Everything is proceeding normally"
Tether's CTO, Paolo Ardoino, disclosed on Twitter the reason for Tether's current value. According to him, nothing is wrong and Tether is simply processing "USDT

redemptions." So if we are to believe Ardoino, the panic surrounding Tether is nothing more than fear, uncertainty & doubt (FUD).

Ardoino also informed The Block Research that there is nothing going on at the moment that investors should be concerned about:

"Tether continues to process redemptions normally amid some expected market panic after yesterday's market. Despite this, Tether has not and will not refuse redemptions to its verified customers, which has always been its practice. In the last 24 hours alone, Tether has honored more than 300 million USDt redemptions and is already processing another 1 billion so far today without any issues."

Stablecoins versus the EU?

If you look at what is available in the world of cryptocurrencies in terms of stablecoins, it is not much. Aside from some stablecoins that copy the value of, say, gold or silver, there are almost only stablecoins on the U.S. dollar. If you are reading this, you probably prefer to use the euro, but it is difficult to get dollars stablecoins. The European Commission is now giving the impression that this will continue.

The answer is NO to large dollars stablecoins
This is what CoinDesk writes, claiming to have seen a report regarding the regulation of stablecoins. The research comes from the European Commission, but has not yet been published. It is a so-called 'non-paper', which does not represent the official position of the commission. With this, it presumably tries to promote discussion, which should result in better regulations. CoinDesk has spoken to two individuals who have confirmed the contents of the report.

Euro-stablecoins, which do not originate from the European Central Bank (ECB), are not being banned outright, according to CoinDesk. Instead, the commission aims to limit stablecoin issuers to a maximum of 1 million transactions per day. The crypto newspaper implies that the market value should further not exceed 200 million euros.

The reason behind the decision

Of course, the report could have as its purpose not only the stimulation of discussions. It could also be that the committee is indicating by this that it does not want large stablecoins. The US does seem to allow these stablecoins for the time being. Currently, tether (USDT) is still the largest stablecoin with a market value of about $82 billion. That is far more than a theoretical limit of 200 million euros.

A dollars variant as large would mean losing face for the ECB. The ECB, of course, issues the dollars and wants to be in control of the dollars itself. Even if a stablecoin has collateral with the same amount of euros, this could reduce the ECB's influence.

Europe is planning to implement "Markets in Crypto Assets Regulation" (MiCA) regulations soon. The fiasco with TerraUSD (UST) and terra (LUNA) could potentially add pressure to this process. The fiasco indicates why some regulators want to regulate stablecoins. There are also ongoing discussions about regulating crypto-based services as banking products.

Dogecoin or Ethereum, what's happening?

According to a recent survey by TRG Datacenters, Ethereum (ETH) is the "most hated" cryptocurrency on Twitter. Dogecoin (DOGE), on the other hand, is the most liked crypto on the social media platform.

TRG Datacenters analyzed Twitter posts between January 2021 and January 2022 to find out which crypto elicited the most emotional responses. However, the study only took a look at five crypto: bitcoin (BTC), ethereum (ETH), litecoin (LTC), cardano (ADA) and dogecoin (DOGE).

Ethereum most hated crypto
The research results show that ethereum received relatively the most negative Tweets last year, namely 29% of the total. Ethereum is especially criticized for its speed (compared to newer "Ethereum killers") and high transaction costs.

An increase in negativity for Ethereum is usually accompanied by an increase in its price. According to the study, this means that some people do not want Ethereum to be a success. Also, an unintended hard fork last year led to a rise in negative sentiment.

Bitcoin followed close behind with the most negative sentiment, accounting for 27% of all tweets. Bitcoin was still by far the most discussed crypto on Twitter. Then follows cardano with 16% of tweets being negative and litecoin with 8%.

Dogecoin most liked crypto
Dogecoin received only 6% negative reports, making it the most liked crypto, although that is somewhat curious. After all, DOGE is a controversial crypto that once originated as a joke. Much of the crypto community was not at all pleased when Tesla CEO Elon Musk tweeted mostly about this crypto.

According to the study, Musk's posts may be precisely why dogecoin is a favorite on the social media platform. Musk, meanwhile, wants to acquire Twitter for a whopping $44 billion. The peak of positive sentiment regarding dogecoin was reached when Musk announced that Tesla is accepting DOGE for merchandise.

Still, we should take this survey with a large grain of salt since it only looked at five crypto. There is a good chance that more controversial crypto like ripple (XRP) is also receiving a lot of negative sentiment. From a new survey, terra (LUNA) would likely currently take the top spot as the most hated crypto.

Why is USDT crashing?

The past few days have been dominated by the complete collapse of Terra (LUNA) and its associated stablecoin UST. UST lost the peg with the US dollar and as a result the price of LUNA collapsed by more than 99%. Immediately, people began to worry about other stablecoins. To the shock of many crypto investors, the value of Tether (USDT) was also below $1 today.

Tether below $1
The collapse of LUNA and UST had a major impact on the crypto market. Yesterday was a fire-red day and most cryptocurrencies fell by double digits. Even bitcoin (BTC) did not manage to hold on and dropped below $29,000. A similar debacle for by far the largest stablecoin, Tether, could throw quite a bit of oil on the fire.

At the time of writing, Tether is trading on most major exchanges, such as Binance, for less than $1. While crypto investors are obviously not waiting for this after yesterday, it is too early to say that anything is really going on. In fact, Tether is now trading for around $0.98, with a bottom of $0.956 on FTX. That's not $1, of course, but it cannot yet be said that Tether has substantially lost the peg with the U.S. dollar.

"Everything is proceeding normally"
Tether's CTO, Paolo Ardoino, disclosed on Twitter the reason for Tether's current value. According to him, nothing is wrong and Tether is simply processing "USDT

redemptions." So if we are to believe Ardoino, the panic surrounding Tether is nothing more than fear, uncertainty & doubt (FUD).

Ardoino also informed The Block Research that there is nothing going on at the moment that investors should be concerned about:

"Tether continues to process redemptions normally amid some expected market panic after yesterday's market. Despite this, Tether has not and will not refuse redemptions to its verified customers, which has always been its practice. In the last 24 hours alone, Tether has honored more than 300 million USDt redemptions and is already processing another 1 billion so far today without any issues."

The whole crypto market is coming down

It was already quite a bloodbath in the cryptocurrency market but apparently that wasn't the worst of it. The crypto prices are taking another big dive and the altcoins are falling a lot harder than bitcoin (BTC) this time. This period is one of the deepest reds in a long time and the total market capitalization of all crypto is down 14% to $1.23 trillion.

Ethereum drops by 20%
Ethereum (ETH) seemed to recover briefly to $2,400 yesterday morning, but then dipped along with bitcoin after the release of the U.S. consumer price index. Ether plummeted all the way to $1,775 today, even below last summer's dip. Yet ETH then made a small bounce back to $1,900, but is still down a hefty 20% today.

TRON holds up a little better
The list of top 10 largest altcoins (excluding stablecoins) is looking slightly different today for the first time in months. Tron (TRX) falls back in this list and held up the best over the past 24 hours. Still, the TRX price is down 6% and now stands at $0.7.

BNB, XRP, DOT, DOGE, AVAX plummet sharply
Binance coin (BNB) makes a small bounce back towards $250, but is still down 19% today. Ripple (XRP) is already down 27% to $0.37. Polkadot (DOT) is 25% in the minus and currently frolicking at $8. Dogecoin (DOGE) is 28% in the minus and closing at $0.076.

Avalanche (AVAX) is 26.5% in the minus and romping at $28.

SOL, ADA, SHIB drop more than 30%
Solana (SOL) is down a whopping 31% and comes in at $43.8. Cardano (ADA) is already 32% in the red and drops to $0.44. Shiba inu (SHIB) is even 31% in the minus and drops to $0.00001 with which it now has a smaller market capitalization than tron.

Crypto top 100 biggest losses
Also aave (AAVE), waves (WAVES), neo (NEO), enjin (ENJ), dash (DASH), pancakeswap (CAKE), and near (NEAR) are all down about 30% today. For internet computer (ICP), decentraland (MANA), and thorchain (RUNE), the figure is 31%. Arweave (AR), zilliqa (ZIL) and polygon (MATIC) are down about 32%. Theta fuel (TFUEL) and convex finance (CVX) are down 37%. Stepn (GMT) is down 38%, graph (GRT) is down 41% and fantom (FTM) is down 43%. eCash is down a whopping 48%.

It's another very red period in the cryptocurrency market and bitcoin (BTC) continues to fall as it does. The price was already in a downward trend due to high fears in traditional financial markets, but the terra (LUNA) incident is causing even more heavy blows.

Bitcoin price drops 10%
The bitcoin price was still approaching $40,0000 a week ago, shortly after the FOMC meeting. By yesterday morning, bitcoin had plummeted all the way to $30,000,

but seemed to be holding there at first. Bitcoin then recovered towards $32,000, but could not break through this yesterday afternoon.

Then the U.S. consumer price index (CPI) figures were published. We already warned at the beginning of the week that the publication of these figures could cause further volatility. Bitcoin then dipped below $30,000 for the first time since last summer.

Still, bitcoin immediately made a small bounce and recovered slightly, but the price did not get beyond $31,650 and began to fall again. By midnight, bitcoin briefly found support around $29,000 and recovered slightly, but that too was short-lived.

Bitcoin then plummeted even deeper and this morning dropped even below $27,000 to a low of $26,600. That's the lowest BTC price since late 2020. Bitcoin is making a bounce back towards $28,000 on KuCoin and $26,550 on Bitvavo at the time of writing. Bitcoin is therefore still 10% down today and 30% down from a week ago.

BTC panic, liquidation, capitulation & disconnection
This means that only investors who bought their BTC more than two years ago are still in profit.

The $27,000 level was seen as a possible bottom of this downtrend. Outside of the dip to $26,600, this boundary is still holding so far. Whether bitcoin can make a trend reversal now, however, is highly uncertain. Fear and panic remain high and we may have to reckon with a further drop to the next limit, around $24,000. There are also already analysts who by now even fear a dip to $20,000.

On Monday 9th of May, the price of Terra's UST stablecoin collapsed. TerraUSD (UST) is unable to maintain its "peg" (linkage) to the U.S. dollar. Terra's currency reserves were simply no longer enough to keep its value equal to the dollar. Janet Yellen, the US Treasury Secretary, took advantage of the situation right away.

Stablecoin regulations now more important than ever The US Financial Stability Oversight Council (FSOC) held a press conference where Yellen spoke alongside Jerome Powell (Federal Reserve) and Gary Gensler (SEC). She seized the opportunity to give stablecoins the thumbs up. Stablecoins need to be regulated quickly, according to Yellen. She sees lack of regulation on stablecoins as a threat to the financial system.

The minister thinks it would be "very appropriate" to be able to start regulating stablecoins by the end of this year. She wants a regulatory framework for stablecoins due to the massive UST crash. The press conference also talks about how stablecoins could be regulated in the same way as money market funds and bank deposits. Those are subject to collateral and liquidity requirements. Furthermore, there are limits on the withdrawal and deposit of money in money market funds and bank accounts. This can prevent the massive shifting of currencies from putting too much pressure on the financial system. Such measures are now absent in the U.S. regarding stablecoins.

In addition to Yellen, politicians such as Senator Pat Toomey, who is usually very positive about cryptocurrencies and defends the small investor, also spoke.

Financial fiasco with TerraUSD (UST)
The press conference came right after the TerraUSD (UST) stablecoin went down hard. Today, the token has fallen even further against the regular dollar. At the time of writing, the price is dropping to just under 30 cents.

Unlike, for example, USDC stablecoin, which uses dollar reserves at U.S. banks, UST relies on algorithms that monitor stability. Earlier this month, the organization behind stablecoin put bitcoin (BTC) on its balance sheet as collateral. This has now fallen in value so hard that the value of UST could no longer be guaranteed.

Bitcoin ETF starts in Australia?

In April 2022, crypto enthusiasts from Australia received positive bitcoin news. Indeed, the country's financial regulator had then approved its first bitcoin exchange-traded fund (ETF). ETFs are exchange-traded funds. A first bitcoin ETF in Australia had been expected for some time and moreover eagerly awaited. As of today, three crypto ETFs are tradable, but this has had an extremely slow start. This has everything to do with the crypto crash we are in the middle of.

The trading volume is very far below the $1 billion that was initially expected. This has a direct connection to the fact that bitcoin is at its lowest point since 2020. The extreme volatility now is making investors not as keen on a bitcoin ETF as was hoped last month.

Bitcoin ETFs in Australia.
The three crypto funds that went live in Australia today are the 21Shares bitcoin (BTC) ETF, their Ethereum (ETH) ETF and the Cosmos Purpose bitcoin ETF. The Cosmos ETF saw trading volume of $400,000 converted in the first hour. The 21Shares bitcoin ETF can put up similar numbers. The ethereum ETF did not get beyond $150,000 in the same time frame. So meager numbers, which do not match the initial expectations.

CEO of Cosmos Asset Management, Dan Annan, also understands and sees that investors are quite cautious at the moment. Still, Annan is hopeful about the long term:

"Investors with a long-term view in terms of exposure to Bitcoin and cryptocurrency will understand that this is a good opportunity for an entry point. Therefore, we hope to see an increase in volumes in the coming days."

To make trading a bit more attractive and in hopes of boosting volumes, Cosmos has decided not to charge a trading fee for the first two months. Incidentally, this decision is also partly due to investors' slight frustration. After all, the bitcoin ETF was actually supposed to go live two weeks ago, but this was unexpectedly delayed.

Bitcoin protected by law in China?

Last year, the Chinese government decided to ban trading in cryptocurrencies, such as bitcoin (BTC) of course, for ordinary citizens. The consequences for the crypto industry were great and most crypto companies left the country. Recently, however, something remarkable took place. Namely, the Shanghai High Court ruled that bitcoin does have economic value and is therefore protected by law.

Bitcoin in China
This became known after the court shared a note on the popular chat platform WeChat, reports Bitcoin.com. This is the first time a court in China has ruled on bitcoin since the ban was introduced by the Chinese government a year ago. This ban was introduced at the time with the aim of supposedly ensuring China's financial stability. The court's ruling reads as follows:

"In the actual trial practice, the People's Court has formed a unanimous opinion on the legal status of bitcoin, identifying it as virtual property [...] Bitcoin has a certain economic value and in accordance with the properties of property, the legal rule of property law is applied for protection."

Implications for the ban
Now, of course, the question remains as to how the government and the crypto industry will react to this monumental ruling. According to a Beijing lawyer, Liu Yang, it could just be that this ruling will be cited in

future cases involving bitcoin and other crypto in the Shanghai region.

So while there is certainly no end in sight to the ban on bitcoin in China, this does show that possibly the controversial ban is in violation of Chinese law.

Indeed, in essence, the ruling states that bitcoin should not have been banned outright. After all, it is protected by law. Whether the Chinese government cares about this remains to be seen. In addition, even higher courts can overturn this ruling by the Shanghai court.

Crypto fraudster sentenced to prison

The United States Department of Justice (DOJ) recently
announced that 25-year-old cryptocurrency trader
Jeremy Spence has been arrested for swindling more
than 170 people. Spence received a prison sentence of
42 months for this. Spence had started a crypto fund
and told his investors that the fund had made a high
profit, but this was not the case at all.

Spence managed the social media accounts of the
investment fund, called Coin Signals. He had to appear
before a New York State judge and confessed his guilt.
Spence additionally received three years of release
under toezcith and must pay damages of more than
$2.8 million to his victims.

Cryptocurrency pyramid scheme
Spence had started the fund with the goal of making a
profit for his investors. However, this did not go entirely
according to plan and his fund only made losses. In an
attempt to hide these losses from his investors, Spence
created fake accounts. With the income from new
investors, he paid out the old investors. This made this
fund look a bit like a pyramid scheme. About $2 million
worth of crypto went around this way.

For example, the 25-year-old fund manager stated in
the fund's online chat group that the fund had made
148% profit, although in reality this was not the case at
all.

Arrested by the FBI
The scammer was eventually caught in January 2021 by the Federal Bureau of Investigation (FBI). Civil charges were also filed by the Commodity Futures Trading Commission (CFTC).

Spence pleaded guilty in November 2021 and was found guilty of commodities fraud for stealing $5 million from unwitting crypto investors from November 2017 to April 2019. In doing so, he made false promises about making a profit when he was actually making a loss.

Yet in court, he expressed regret for his actions and apologized. He said he "came into a world that [he] was totally unprepared for."

ApeCoin is the cryptocurrency associated with the Bored Ape Yacht Club ecosystem, among others. ApeCoin falls into the memecoins category, and these generally exhibit more volatility than the rest of the market.

ApeCoin (APE) recovers

The decline before the recovery
Especially when compared to larger coins like bitcoin and ether. This week was a volatile one for APE, as on May 11 it lost 81 percent of its value in a short period of time. The ApeCoin price dropped from around $11 to $5 on that day.

However, the price has since recovered quite a bit and ApeCoin is trading at around $9. Which is an impressive recovery, but it's not really hopeful that the project can surrender more than 80 percent of its value in a single day.

ApeCoin's impressive rebound
On May 12, ApeCoin already recovered by almost 45 percent to $7.30 and optimism cautiously returned to the community. Meanwhile, the restoration of confidence will be complete with the rebound to $9. However, this still leaves ApeCoin far from the all-time high of $27.50 that it reached on April 28 of this year.

The zigzag movement of the ApeCoin price seemed to broadly follow the rest of the market. As a result of the collapse of UST and the Terra ecosystem, confidence in the market took a big hit. This caused tremendous chaos in the market and ApeCoin could not escape that sentiment either. In addition, the U.S. Federal Reserve, the world's leading central bank, is still pretty hawkish.

Hawkish means that they are looking for ways to tame inflation and plan to raise interest rates, among other things. At the last FOMC meeting, Chairman Jerome Powell announced his intention to raise interest rates again by 0.5 percent at least for the next two meetings. It is not a certainty, however, because Powell indicates that he wants to be able to react dynamically to any changing circumstances.

9.63 dollar possible major resistance
At the moment, the weather is briefly in favor of the Ape ecosystem and the ApeCoin price has the wind in its sails. However, there is important resistance at $9.63 0as that is where the 0.618 Fibonacci line lies. Around that point the price also failed earlier today. There is a chance that the price will continue to move towards that price and encounter resistance at that point.

If ApeCoin breaks through, the way to a higher price is open. However, everything depends on the rest of the market. Indeed, as for many other altcoins, the ApeCoin price shows a high correlation with the bitcoin price. If bitcoin is struggling, then there is little chance that coins like ApeCoin will go through the roof though. Bitcoin, in turn, is dependent on the unpredictable macroeconomic environment we currently find ourselves in. The likelihood of further interest rate increases, high inflation and geopolitical turmoil are generally not good for investments.

Warren Buffet gets free bitcoin?

Investment legend Warren Buffet who is now well into his nineties and known as a great opponent of bitcoin has an indirect bitcoin investment to his name. This is because Berkshire Hathaway, Buffet's investment firm, has a large position in Brazil's Nubank, which has decided to invest 1 percent of its reserves in bitcoin.

It remains to be seen how happy Buffet is with this news, as he once called bitcoin rat poison squared. In 2021, Berkshire Hathaway invested $1 billion (€950 million) in Nubank. So with that, Buffet now indirectly owns bitcoin. However, it cannot be a big surprise for Buffet and cronies, as Nubank is known as a bitcoin-friendly bank.

The statement from Nubank
Nubank says this is to reinforce the company's belief in the current and future potential of bitcoin. The Brazilian bank is using Paxos' service to offer customers the opportunity to buy bitcoin. As a result, Nubank customers cannot send their bitcoin from the platform to their own wallet.

However, the bank plans to add that option in the future. Currently, this option is still in the testing phase, with a few percent of the bank's customers already having that option. Nubank expects to add the option to send bitcoin to a private wallet for all customers in the coming months. So until then, most Nubank customers are forced to keep their bitcoin within Nubank.

Bitcoin is the strongest
The reason Nubank chose bitcoin as a reserve asset on its balance sheet is bitcoin's market share. The largest cryptocurrency still holds 40 percent of the market and is therefore seen as the most secure option crypto has to offer. With the investment, Nubank looks to definitively establish itself as a bitcoin-friendly bank. In addition to buying bitcoin through its normal trading platform, customers can also invest in the Brazilian bitcoin ETF.

Painful moment for Warren Buffet?
It remains to be seen to what extent Warren Buffet knew about these plans. After all, not long ago the seasoned and successful investor was still shouting that he wouldn't buy all the bitcoin in the world for $25 yet and that bitcoin has no value. A major investment from Berkshire Hathaway clearly does not share that opinion with Buffet and is instead betting ever larger on bitcoin.

Nubank's shares are for sale on the New York Stock Exchange, among others, and the market seems at least satisfied with the bank's bitcoin investment. That satisfaction will not be based on bitcoin's current stock price performance, which can be called fairly dramatic. After the Terra drama, the bitcoin price has now fallen back to just over 26,000 euros.

New difficulty for bitcoin mining?

Bitcoin (BTC) miners are probably going to notice the crash of bitcoin in the near future. In fact, the network's difficulty was adjusted yesterday to a record high. In short, mining BTC has never been more difficult, while the price has thus plummeted.

Bitcoin difficulty to record
Since July 2021, the Bitcoin network's computing power was in an obvious upward trend. The computational difficulty took a huge hit just before that after China imposed a ban on mining. More and more miners from other parts of the world joined the network afterwards after it became clear that it can be a pretty lucrative business. And over the past year, this attraction was mainly due to the rising bitcoin price.

To ensure that on average a block of transactions is added to the blockchain every 10 minutes, the network automatically balances itself using the difficulty adjustment. This adjustment takes place every 2,016 blocks. If the block time during this period was on average less than 10 minutes, the difficulty is increased. In this way, the work of miners becomes more difficult and the blocking times should return to 10 minutes.

After the steady upward trend of computing power, which also reached a record in early May, the difficulty increased by 4.9% yesterday. It has never been so difficult for miners to mine bitcoins!

Miners are going to feel pain after bitcoin crash
Although this indicates that the network is also
extremely secure, it is possible that BTC miners are
going to have a tough time. With the falling bitcoin
price, it is becoming less and less profitable to mine.

It is therefore likely that the hashrate will begin to
decline in the near future. This decrease will of course
eventually make it easier to mine bitcoins as the
difficulty will also decrease.

The future of bitcoin in Brazil

Nubank, Brazil's largest bank, announced on May 11 that it will give its clients the ability to trade bitcoin (BTC) and ethereum (ETH). The bank indicated that clients will be able to trade in these two cryptocurrencies for a minimum of 1 Brazilian real. Previously, clients could already invest in cryptocurrencies at this bank, however, they could only do so by means of exchange traded funds (ETFs).

Strong growth in popularity of BTC and ETH
David Vélez, CEO and co-founder of Nubank, said that cryptocurrencies have grown strongly in popularity. In addition, he indicated that cryptocurrencies can change the world.

Nubank is the largest fintech bank in Latin America. In addition, this bank only functions as an online bank and offers many different innovative products and services. The bank works within different companies, and entities such as Sequoia Capital and Berkshire Hathaway invest in Nubank.

Clients do not need to create a special account but can just use their current account to buy these cryptocurrencies. This is a great advantage as it ensures that these users can enter the market more easily.

Cryptocurrencies are very popular in Latin America. Some countries allow more regarding this sector than others, however, we can clearly see that more and more banks are embracing cryptocurrencies.

Nubank's good timing

Alternatively, this decision by the bank may have come at the wrong time. The price of bitcoin has corrected hard in recent days, even touching $26,700 and ethereum dropped to a bottom of $1,700.

It is currently not a good time for the launch of crypto related products or services. Another product that will appear on the market is Australia's first bitcoin ETF. This ETF will come to market on May 12.

Taxes on BTC in Germany

The crypto market is bleeding, but developments surrounding the sector continue! In Germany, more has now become clear about how cryptocurrencies like bitcoin (BTC) and ethereum (ETH) are treated by tax authorities. And it's especially good bitcoin news for Germans.

Germans won't have to pay tax on bitcoin after 1 year The German Ministry of Finance recently published the very first guidelines regarding the taxation of cryptocurrencies. This is a 24-page document that touches on all kinds of issues regarding crypto.

Among other things, this document shows that people who invest in bitcoin, ethereum or similar cryptocurrencies do not have to pay tax on them after one year. Bitcoins sold after one year are therefore not subject to profit tax.

By the way, this also applies to income from staking and crypto lending services. Staking is the passive earning of crypto in a proof-of-stake (PoS) network like Cardano (ADA). Previously, there was talk that the one-year term would be extended to 10 years once an investor uses the crypto within a lending service or to strike, but that is not the case, according to Parliamentary State Secretary Katja Hessel:

"For individuals, the sale of purchased bitcoin and ether is tax free after one year. The deadline is not extended to ten years if, for example, bitcoin has previously been used for loans or if the taxpayer has provided ether as a stake to someone else to create his block."

Positive development for crypto
The new guidelines are positive for crypto because there is still a lot of ambiguity surrounding the sector. Crypto is new and so there is still a lot to work on. Therefore, Hessel states that this document will certainly not be the last:

"Of course, the upcoming official publication of the BMF letter is not the end of our discussion on the subject, but an interim result. The rapid development of the 'crypto world' ensures that we will not run out of topics. An additional letter on the obligations to cooperate and register is already underway."

Microstrategy and Bitcoin

MicroStrategy led by CEO Michael Saylor is one of the largest holders of bitcoin (BTC) in the world. The company has many billions in bitcoin on its balance sheet and is also traded on the US stock exchange. Investors in MicroStrategy did start to get a little worried after bitcoin's steep price drops. According to Saylor, however, the company will only really be in trouble if bitcoin crashes all the way to around $3,000.

Michael Saylors bitcoin loans
Especially MicroStrategy's bitcoin positions that were bought with a loan could be at risk, or so investors thought. As a result, rumors were flying that MicroStrategy would be liquidated if bitcoin dropped to the $21,000 mark, which would be far from out of the question today.

This is cause for concern because the company's subsidiary, MacroStrategy, took out a $205 million loan from Silvergate Bank in March 2022, using some of MicroStrategy's bitcoin as collateral for the debt. MicroStrategy then used the proceeds to pursue the company's BTC strategy.

If the price of BTC got too low, it would trigger a margin call on the Silvergate loan because the value of the collateral would fall. This was a central point in the company's earnings call in May where the company's CFO, Phone Le, confirmed that the company would have to sell some bitcoin if the price of BTC fell below $21,000.

BTC bottom price of $3,500

According to Saylor, however, it is not that simple. In fact, he states that MicroStrategy holds over 115,000 bitcoins that they could make available as collateral in the event that bitcoin drops to the $21,000 mark.

Only when bitcoin completely collapses to $3,562 will MicroStrategy really have a problem and they will be forced to sell their bitcoin holdings. Fortunately, it is still a long way off and it remains to be seen whether this scenario is realistic.

KuCoin worth $10 billion after $150 million investment

Deeper into Web 3.0: Wallets, DeFi, NFT & GameFi
KuCoin plans to use the new capital to further expand its services and, in particular, go deeper into Web 3.0. The exchange will invest in crypto wallets, decentralized finance (DeFi), non-fungible token (NFT) platforms and GameFi, among others. The latter is a relatively new combination of blockchain gaming and finance.

The Series B funding round was led by Jump Crypto and saw multiple investment firms participate, including Circle Ventures, IDG Capital and Matrix Partners. Tak Fujishima of Jump Crypto said the following:

"KuCoin offers a comprehensive platform of crypto services to a global audience, which is one of the many reasons we are proud to lead this round. We are excited to support the company as it continues to grow and expand its offerings in futures and margin trading, lending, strike and passive returns to support the growth of Web 3.0 and the crypto markets."

Improving KuCoin's performance and security.
In addition, KuCoin will use part of the new investment to improve the exchange's trading system. The press release talks about a tenfold performance improvement that will allow the trading platform to better serve its 18 million customers. KuCoin also plans to improve the security of the trading platform.

"The confidence of prominent investors, including Jump Crypto and Circle Ventures, reinforces our vision that one day everyone will be involved with crypto. KuCoin was built for all classes of investors, and we believe these new investors and partners will help make KuCoin synonymous with a safe and secure gateway to the crypto world."

Says Johnny Lyu, CEO of KuCoin. KuCoin wants KCC, the public blockchain built by KuCoin's community, to be a central part of this decentralized ecosystem.

Bitcoin makes strong recovery

Bitcoin (BTC) and the cryptocurrency market in general have been hit hard in recent days. The prices were already in a downward trend, but the fiasco surrounding terra (LUNA) resulted in a deep red market.

Still, bitcoin was able to recover over the past 24 hours. The market is reacting with some relief and sentiment is cautiously becoming slightly more positive. Nevertheless, fear and uncertainty is still very high and bitcoin could still fall deeper.

Bitcoin price recovers by 10%
The bitcoin price arrived at the $27,000 mark yesterday morning, May the 13th. Although bitcoin first made another dip towards $26,600, and on some exchanges even towards $25,000, this boundary around $27,000 is holding for now.

Bitcoin then began to rise. The price first encountered some resistance around $28,000, but was able to break through it yesterday afternoon. The $29,000 also offered some resistance for a while, but bitcoin broke through that as well by yesterday evening.

Next, bitcoin was rejected around $29,800, but the price then held firm above $28,000 and was able to rise again after that. Bitcoin peaked at $30,885 this morning and at the time of writing is trading at $30,300 on KuCoin and €29,000 on Bltvavo. This puts the price at a whopping 10% plus today.

Bitcoin investors try to aim for bottom
It is possible that bitcoin has reached its bottom around this $27,000 and is now starting a recovery. Volume is finally starting to increase in the last few hours which may indicate a return of confidence.

However, this is far from certain. In order to speak of a trend reversal, the price must now first climb out of a very deep gap. It is possible that bitcoin may already run into too much resistance around $32,000 and then resume its downward trend.

Then we may have to reckon with a test of the $24,000 mark. It is notable that investors are currently trying to aim exactly at the bottom. If so, it is usually virtually impossible.

If you are investing for the long term and still have full confidence in bitcoin, then it also makes little difference to target exactly the bottom. If you have less confidence and/or are trading for the short term, then it might be wise to wait for a stronger sign of a trend reversal first. "Don't catch a falling knife" is therefore a well-known saying for investors; prices can always fall deeper.

Meanwhile, the futures market finally cooled down, but unfortunately it was accompanied by a big crash. Open interest is currently at its lowest in seven months, a clear sign of the uncertainty.

Despite this, large amounts of longs on Bitfinex are currently being closed and this may actually indicate a return of confidence.

Should you invest in crypto now?

If you've followed the news a bit in recent years, you know better than anyone that interest in Bitcoin has skyrocketed. Since the beginning of the corona crisis, many have made an investment in crypto.

Large growth in number of investors due to pandemic To see if crypto is a must for 2022, it is good to first look at the years before. Indeed, there is a clear reason why interest in Bitcoin and other altcoins has risen within a short period of time. Corona caused us all to rearrange our daily lives for a period of time. One lockdown wasn't finished yet or another lockdown was already at the door. From nowhere, people had to stay home a lot, which meant spending less money. At the same time, they saw that cryptocurrencies were doing very well; since the beginning of the pandemic, there was an upward trend there.

With extra money in their account, many people decided to take the plunge. The prices kept rising during the pandemic and the news coverage about crypto remained positive. What should also be taken into account, is the fact that the savings rate is currently very low. This means that you will get almost nothing for the savings you leave in the bank. In fact, in many cases there is a greater chance that you will earn more with it when you put it into crypto - provided, of course, that you are aware of exactly how crypto works. All of these factors combined provide the right foundation for taking a look at the crypto world.

What you need to know about investing in crypto
Many novice investors wonder if they will be able to make a good amount of money from their efforts in cryptocurrency within a short period of time. The answer to that is: generally speaking, no. Investing in crypto is most profitable when you invest for the longer term. This means that buying Bitcoin should only be done with money that can be missed for a time and that you therefore do not need immediately. In fact, past practice has shown that the value of Bitcoin and other coins has started to rise over the years. Of course, it can happen that your bet is suddenly worth a lot one day or that its value has plummeted.

It is important not to act on emotion at such a time, but to stick to a clear strategy that will help you make money in the long run. The value of Bitcoin today is so high for a reason; there have been many ups and downs. However, the fact is that Bitcoin once started with a value of $ 0. In 2010, two pizzas were even paid for with 10,000 Bitcoin. That is hard to imagine now that one Bitcoin has topped that amount multiple times. Experts expect Bitcoin and other crypto to become the currency of the future, so it certainly can't hurt to prepare for it now.

Crypto in 2022: to invest or not to invest?
Therefore, it is definitely recommended to start investing in cryptocurrency in 2022, should you have the money to do so and should your interest lie there. Several traders, brokers and professionals in the field of

crypto expect that 2022 will be an interesting year for the prices. In fact, it already is; due to Russia's attacks in Ukraine, we are seeing a lot of ups and downs on the Bitcoin price. You never know what else is going to happen and how that will affect cryptocurrencies. That is the only "downside" to investing in this virtual money; it is incredibly volatile.

However, if you take that into account when you start investing in crypto, this year is definitely a good time to start. In recent years, rising prices have proven a lot. Chances are that things will only get better in the coming period on the various exchange rates. Remember that one day may go better than the next and that you should not invest with money that you immediately need. Only then is investing in Bitcoin or any other crypto currency fun and exciting and more importantly profitable.

Best crypto currencies 2022
The world's number one crypto currency, Bitcoin, needs no announcement as an investment option. Even for 2022, it remains the best coin to buy now. But what else can you invest in in 2022? Stellar Lumens, XLM, can also be considered a good coin to buy now. XLM may have had a turbulent 2020, but now it is trading near its ATH. Moreover, there are some great projects planned on the horizon.

For example, Stellar Lumens itself recently invested $5 million in Wyre, a leading blockchain payment service. This investment will provide XLM, access to currency pairs. Furthermore, Stellar has been chosen by the Ukrainian Central Bank to contribute to the development of their own CBDC, central bank digital currency.

The second largest cryptocurrency we should definitely not forget about in 2022, Ethereum. ETH is especially important for developers to develop and run various applications on the Ethereum platform. The market size of Ethereum is about 19% of that of Bitcoin. Therefore, Ethereum can certainly also be called the best crypto currency to invest in.

One of the options for 2022 is also Dogecoin. It was launched as a joke by two programmers. Nevertheless, Doge enjoys attention from influential influencers, such as Musk of Tesla, Gene Simmons of rock band Kiss and rapper Snoop Dogg.

Best crypto to buy in 2022
What is the best crypto coin in 2022 to buy even more? Another crypto coin that you can consider best for investment in 2022 is Litecoin. Using LTC as its token, based on Bitcoin, Litecoin was launched in 2011 by Charlie Lee. Litecoin is often referred to as the silver of gold Bitcoin. Litecoin shares many similarities with Bitcoin. However, LTC has a faster block rate and therefore offers a faster transaction confirmation time.

Less popular among developers, but the number of sellers accepting LTC is growing. LTC has a market capitalization of $13 billion at the time of writing.

Cryptocurrency DOT from creator Polkadot is expected to become more interesting in 2022. Connecting authorized and permissionless blockchains as well as oracles will further attract this system. The goal is to allow different networks to cooperate with each other without compromising security. By the way, that is one advantage of Polkadot compared to Ethereum.

You can create your own blockchain on Ethereum with your own token, but you will also have to build in your own security. Whereas on Polkadot you can use shared security.

More and more investors and traders are becoming interested in crypto currencies and in particular in Bitcoin. Many people have the intention to actually step into the crypto world but have no idea when to do so. Should you let yourself be led by the success stories or is it perhaps better not to? In this article you will discover the answer.

Opportunities to invest in Bitcoins

The increased interest in crypto currencies has ensured that there are also plenty of opportunities to invest in Bitcoins. Where in the past you could only go to foreign websites for this, nowadays you can also go to different organizations in the Netherlands. There are several (Dutch) exchanges and by using the services of an organization such as Bitcoin Pro you can even apply a trading bot to them. This will take some of the work out of trading Bitcoins for you.

How interesting is a Bitcoin investment?

Based on the media reports, Bitcoin investment is very interesting. You only have to do a quick search to read several success stories about it. Although these stories are very interesting and even inspire many people to make a Bitcoin investment themselves, the risks involved should not be ignored. After all, Bitcoin prices are subject to considerable change. It is not excluded that huge peaks in the price can alternate with sharp price drops. While this can create risk, it also provides a good opportunity to determine the best time to make a Bitcoin investment.

Buy low, sell high

When talking about the best time to invest in cryptocurrency, the term "buy low, sell high" quickly comes to mind. After all, a common mistake is to choose a Bitcoin investment when the price is very high. After all, many people are inspired by the aforementioned success stories spread by the various media. To maximize your return on investment, it is better to invest when the Bitcoin price is at its lowest and sell when it is at its highest. In addition, it is a wise choice to spread the investment. This can be done by making the investment itself in multiple parts or by choosing multiple cryptocurrencies to invest in. The above points out that it is very important to keep a close eye on the crypto prices and all the world news to determine the best time for a Bitcoin investment.

The enormous bitcoin hype in 2018

Thinking back on it puts a very big smile on my face. It was summer 2018 when I first started to delve into Bitcoin. And specifically blockchain technology. The very first article I read was about Bitcoin. At the time, I could see the potential of this digital currency, but I didn't quite believe in it. However, the second article I read after that caught my full attention. The second article was about the blockchain, the technology behind Bitcoin. Very fascinating is this technology, which is based on decentralization and high traceability within the blockchain. I was convinced, and decided to make my very first investment. Only not to invest in Bitcoin, but in Ethereum.

Nowadays, there are many finance websites where you can buy Bitcoin. But back then in the summer of 2018, there were only a few websites where you could do this. Often you then had to save the blockchain code on a USB or on paper. Not surprisingly, so many people lost his or her codes, along with all their Bitcoins! Now that is thankfully a thing of the past. Anyway, back then I bought my first Ethereum coins. I had bought four coins for 100 dollars each. Let's forget for a moment the fact that I was still a huge amateur at the time and had committed many of the pitfalls for novice investors. But sometimes luck is with the stupid, and that was true for me at the time. Because apparently, I had gotten in just before the huge Bitcoin hype. And yes, that brought me tremendously high returns.

How my first Ethereum investment had a return of +900%

When I had bought Ethereum, I had also bought some other cryptocurrency. And then it all started. Sometime in September and October 2018, the Bitcoin Hype hit. One cryptocurrency after another skyrocketed. For example, at the peak of the hype, my Ethereum coins were worth 1000 dollars each. I had bought them for 100 euros, and so that's a 900% return. I had also bought some Litecoin coins that had flown from 50 dollars to 250 euros. And one of my best investments was Verge. With Verge, I had made a whopping 5,000 dollars from 100 euros. But as I said, I was a total amateur at the time and made a lot of mistakes.

Fortunately, I didn't do everything wrong. For example, I had only invested with money I could spare. That's one of the most important rules of getting rich with investing: only invest with money you can miss. I had invested a total of about 1500 euros. And at some point this was worth about 13,000 euros. Yes, that's a tremendously high return in just four months. Unfortunately, my biggest mistake was that I got completely caught up in the hype. I forgot something very important: collecting profits. All this time I had been holding my cryptocurrency, even to this day. Fortunately, the price is going back up a bit, but it will be years before we get back to 2018 levels.

Moral of the story: should you invest in a hype, make sure you pocket your profits in time. Because before you know it, it may be too late and you will be left empty-handed.

But note: not collecting my profits was not the biggest mistake.

Bitcoin's lack of Use Case and Value in 2018.
The biggest mistake I made in 2018 was investing in hype. Lots of people have become millionaires investing in Bitcoin. And I'm not ruling out the possibility of many more millionaires in the coming years thanks to Bitcoin. But the big difference between me and those millionaires, is that all those Bitcoin millionaires got there very early. They were already investing in the potential of this digital currency from 2013. Back then, you could invest in Bitcoin for under a euro! In such a case, it may be worth the gamble to invest, say, 500 dollars in something that may have enormous potential. That's always better than putting 500 dollars on black or red at the Casino....

Bitcoin was all hype in 2018. At that time it only had potential, but there was no tangible Value behind it. Nor did it have a strong Use Case. The latter is that a technology also has useful applications in practice. Bitcoin still has no value in 2022. You can hardly use it anywhere, and the exchange rate still fluctuates far too much making it not a valid means of payment. This makes Bitcoin not a smart investment in my eyes.

For me, a smart investment is an investment in something tangible that actually generates revenue and especially profit. Think about real estate funds that reap huge profits every month thanks to rent money. Or think about growth stocks of emerging popular companies. As companies grow more and more each year thanks to an increasing customer base, they will also generate more and more sales and profits. This makes a company worth more. The greater the growth potential of a company, the more valuable it is. This also applies to industries. Some industries grow faster than others. Therefore, investing in growth markets is a very logical and smart investment. We often see this value reflected in the stock price. Then a stock is relatively "expensive." But if you are lucky, you will find valuable stocks that have a relatively "cheap" price. This way of investing is also called Value Investing.

Is it safe or not to invest in Bitcoin and cryptocurrency?

Meanwhile, the platforms on which you can buy Bitcoins are getting better and more user-friendly. One example of this is Satos. This is the best rated cryptocurrency trading platform in Europe. A very important development here is protection. The trading platforms of 2022 have much better security than was the case in 2018 and even earlier. Back then, there were all kinds of stories in the media about Bitcoins being stolen by hackers. Fortunately, that is more and more a thing of the past (and especially if you are a small investor). The security is now comparable to normal investment platforms. Unfortunately, the reality is that Bitcoins are more likely to be hacked than a normal investment portfolio of stocks (which are rarely hacked). So yes, it has become more secure but still not as secure as "normal" investments.

When is it good to invest in crypto?
If reality is to be believed, it can be said that it is a good idea to invest in crypto. This is especially the case if you are someone who wants to get direct exposure regarding the actual demand for this type of currency.

At the same time, the idea of buying stocks exposed to digital currency is a lot less risky. It may end up coming with fewer benefits, but you certainly don't have to be on the edge because you are extremely volatile.

Risks associated with crypto-currencies

When it comes to discussing the risks, there are several. Let's not just favor crypto by considering it free from all kinds of problems. On the contrary, there are some factors that you should be well aware of before deciding whether or not to invest in crypto.

Vulnerability to cyber attacks

- Fierce competition
- Possible future stringent regulations
- Vulnerability to cyber attacks

Unlike stock markets, crypto exchanges are quite vulnerable to cyber attacks. Because this currency is digital and completely intangible, it can be hacked. There is a good chance that it could become the target of all kinds of criminal activities. Even some of the biggest investors have fallen prey to these targets in the past.

Therefore, they have lost a significant amount of investment due to these attackers. Much of their digital currency was stolen because there was a security breach halfway through a crypto exchange.

Although using techniques to analyze the bitcoin market makes things pretty secure, you still cannot guarantee 100% income from your investments.

Storing crypto is a pretty difficult process. In comparison, owning bonds is considered a lot easier. This vulnerability of digital currencies has really deterred many people from investing in them.

Fierce competition

The competition in the field of crypto is cutthroat. Even though the risk is high, people trust it and buy in en masse. The industry-backed blockchain is growing with each passing day. The entire infrastructure is built on digital and the crypto ecosystem is gaining a lot of momentum.

So when it comes to buying crypto, you may be facing a lot of competition. Its value may increase the moment you decide to buy it to the moment you get your hands on it. So making quick decisions and staying on track is indeed necessary.

Possible future stringent regulations

With governments and international institutions becoming increasingly aware of the importance of cryptocurrency, there is a chance of strict regulations for the industry in the future. Even the IMF experts have called for a better level of industry regulation, showing that this could be possible in the future.

Investing in crypto as a business owner?

Investing in crypto is becoming increasingly well-known among consumers, but companies are also able to find their way to the exchange. However, an organization must meet other requirements and undergo a strict verification process. Also take into account that you have to pay taxes and that you sometimes have to convert your crypto assets into euros, so that the correct profit or loss balance can be determined. In this article, I'll take you through how to invest in cryptocurrencies as a business and what the implications are.

Investing in crypto in 2022
You would like to invest in crypto with your business assets. In this article I'm going to tell you how, but let's start at the beginning. What investing in crypto in 2022, is that actually smart?

We are in a special situation right now, because all kinds of things are going on in the world. We are living at a rapid pace towards a new financial system, there is an awful lot of scarcity in the commodities market, wars are breaking out and our climate is anything but stable. To say that it is chaos is an understatement.

Fickle prices in the crypto market are fortunately quite normal. We don't call it a "volatile" market for nothing; gross fluctuations are not strange and this is what you need to be prepared for. Ultimately, every drop or rise is a reaction to an event or trend in the market, which is therefore quite logical. You can't profit from the ups if there are no downs, that's just how it works.

Last week I also wrote an article about what you can do with your money in uncertain times and my colleague Christiaan wrote about how to invest your wealth in gold. Gold also does well in times when the dollar is falling.

Store your digital coins safely
Once you have purchased them, your coins are on the exchange. That is not a safe place to store them, because in case of a hack or a crash, you have lost everything. Of course, that's not what you want for your business assets. Here are the options you have:

Hosted wallet - This is a wallet that is often already created by the exchange itself, when you buy your currencies. For example, if you buy Ethereum (ETH) through Bitvavo, your funds will go directly into such a wallet. This is obviously secure, but by far not the safest option;

Software wallet - A software wallet is an online environment in which you store your cryptos. You download this wallet onto your computer or into an app on your device. You are the only one who has these login details, and there is no third party involved, but it is still not the safest option;

Hardware wallet - This is an option I would recommend myself. Through a hardware wallet, such as the Ledger, you are assured that everything is actually under your control. This saves you the worry and prevents you from losing your coins in a hack or crash.

How to find the right coins?
Please note: this is a side note to make your search for the right digital coins easier. It is not financial advice and absolutely no way of telling you, what you should invest in. It is entirely up to you to decide what to invest in and how to go about it. Do your own research!

These are guidelines for finding the right investment option for you:

Use a reliable, secure exchange that fits your needs; Enjoy the fact that with crypto, you can often (note: not always) achieve returns that you absolutely cannot achieve with savings;

You can go for a certain number of coins or create a broad portfolio. Do you go for a bit of everything, do you go specifically for DeFi or do you stick to a few altcoins?

Look carefully at what your options are. Are you going to buy and HODL, so save for the long term? Do you want to buy in a dip and sell in a peak? Do you want to strike?

Some exchanges offer entrepreneurs special bonuses, pre-sale offers or deals so that they will invest in crypto more and more often. Should this be right up your alley, take advantage of it!

Benefit as a company from current crypto trends
As a business, do you want to do more than just invest in the cryptocurrencies? Maybe you even want to run a business or project that is entirely active in this industry! Or do you want to know how to pay as little tax on your crypto assets, in a legal way of course.

Business investment in crypto can definitely be worthwhile. Yes, you need to know what you're doing and yes, you also need to keep good records. But that is also the case without crypto investments. If you use a reliable exchange, create a business account and store your purchased digital coins safely, this can give you a nice return.

It is good to know that besides investing in crypto, you can also start a business in the world of crypto. Think about making NFTs, advising people or founding a project on the blockchain. Whatever you are planning, and whatever your ambitions are, the crypto world is at your feet. I wish you the best of luck and fun!

Investing in the Cardano exchange rate in 2022

One of the coins that experts expect a lot of in the coming years is the ADA on the Cardano exchange rate. While no one can predict the course of cryptocurrency, this is for a reason. The team behind Cardano is hard at work renewing and improving the network, which is directly reflected in the prices. For example, in March 2020 the currency was only worth $0.03 and we see that in August 2021 the ADA had a value of $2.61. Experts expect the Cardano exchange rate to remain quiet at the beginning of 2022 before experiencing a rise. It is particularly the longer term, think 2023 to 2025, that makes investing in Cardano interesting.

Which cryptocurrency shows promise?

Crypto has become a growing sensation in recent years; the speed at which crypto has become a trend has been faster than the adoption of the Internet itself, and the end is far from in sight. Crypto is hot, crypto is trending, and a lot of money is going into it. The crypto forecast 2022 is therefore positively expected by many investors, and finding the best coins is becoming increasingly difficult. More and more small crypto with potential are emerging. Also, more and more crypto exchanges and marketplaces are emerging.

By the end of 2025, it is expected that there will be about one billion global Bitcoin wallets. This figure is expected to continue to rise due to the global reach of the Internet, and the many countries that are beginning to accept Bitcoin as a legal tender.

New crypto currencies 2022
But it is not only Bitcoin that is growing, but also other crypto currencies such as Ethereum, whose trend since 2019 has developed faster than Bitcoin's. The growth of Decentralized finance (DeFi) is even more impressive, with the number of users tripling since the beginning of 2021. This "risky" market has attracted more investors, and as 2021 reaches its final quarter, investors are now looking for the best crypto investments in 2022. Which coin is going to rise in 2022 depends mainly on the projects it represents. Which new crypto coins will take over 2022 we can see through the examples below.

Crypto expectation 2022
The crypto markets are more volatile than the stock markets, which makes it even more important as an investor to study the different cryptocurrencies well, and what the longer-term plan is for the projects behind the crypto currency. In this chapter, we will discuss the top 8 crypto coins 2022 outside of Bitcoin, so that you as an investor can make a thoughtful choice for your investment portfolio in 2022. Don't just delve into the crypto price, but also the right type of crypto exchange can make a lot of difference in your investing experience. Even if the crypto forecast 2022 is positive, be sure before you invest money. Keep yourself updated with the latest crypto news on websites like marketupdate.co.uk and exchanges like Binance.

The best crypto coins 2022 to invest in
The following crypto currencies are projects that are running well and of which there is a high expectation for crypto 2022. Especially for investors who are looking for a longer term investment, these crypto currencies are a good choice to get more involved in. We do not give financial advice, but share this information passed on the results of the past months, along with the longer term plan for the project. Just make sure yourself that you thoroughly immerse yourself in a crypto before you decide to invest.

Litecoin as an investment for 2022

Besides the good Cardano news, there are other coins in which you can invest in 2022. Litecoin, for example, is one of them. This crypto currency is also seen as the alternative to Bitcoin. This is because they both operate on the same kind of network, namely the blockchain. One of the big advantages of Litecoin is that it has proven to be a very solid coin in the past (and present). This makes investing in it all the more interesting. In addition, unlike Bitcoin, the currency does not have to deal with high transaction costs. This may well work in favor of this altcoin in the coming years. Therefore, definitely keep an eye on Litecoin in 2022 and add the coin to your investment portfolio.

Invest in XRP from Ripple in 2022

In conclusion, it can certainly bring the necessary benefit when you start investing in XRP from Ripple in 2022. Ripple is impossible to imagine the crypto world without it. In recent years, this crypto currency has become much more valuable making it a good currency for business investing. Although few prominent people in crypto dare to speak out about the coin, there are some trading companies that expect Ripple to double in value compared to 2021. Others even expect an even higher value on the Ripple price. Never go entirely by these kinds of expectations, but see for yourself what the best choice is in terms of investing in cryptocurrency for your business. Nobody can really predict the future of crypto currencies like the Cardano exchange rate.

Ethereum [ETH] 2022

Ethereum is an on decentralized blockchain network with its own crypto coin to pay with, the cryptocurrency Ether (ETH). Ethereum is a top contender because of its smart contract functionality. Smart contracts are like paper contracts that are executed when all conditions are met, but without an intermediary such as a bank or other middleman. Various developers are using the Ethereum network to create various projects, such as decentralized exchanges (DEXs), security tokens (which can replace paper certificates and other financial products), non-replaceable tokens (NFTs) that are used to replace art and other valuable items, such as as as well as creating new cryptocurrencies entirely with Ethereum's ERC-20 token standard.

Ethereum is currently switching its consensus mechanism to a Proof of Stake (PoS) of its PoW mechanism with the ETH2.0 upgrade. Stakers can now offer their ETH as a deposited investment for additional passive income. This is not only for additional return but also better for the environment. After all, old-fashioned mining consumes a lot of energy.

What makes Ethereum a good investment?
Ethereum is the largest blockchain network for decentralized applications and has the second largest market capitalization behind Bitcoin.

With decentralized apps and the ERC-20 token standard, Ethereum offers many opportunities for different projects and is the leading choice for the development of new crypto currencies.

Ether is the only coin being discussed to surpass bitcoin in the near term, and all dApps, smart contracts, security tokens, NFTs and many other products require them to run on the ETH blockchain.

ETH has shown strong capacity since 2015, and it is still evolving to get better. For example, there is the ongoing ETH2.0 upgrade which contributes to a much more efficient and faster PoS consensus mechanism and system of Shards. ETH is still one of the best crypto currencies 2022 .

Strike is an additional income generator (about 8% per year) for investors who want to hold ETH and earn an additional return. At Binance you can strike ETH and other crypto coins.

Polkadot [DOT] 2022

Polkadot is a proprietary blockchain network that has connected different blockchains that have different functions, to make them work together. Polkadot allows developers, like Ethereum, to build apps and smart contracts. Polkadot's relay chains enable communication of dApps with other blockchain networks. Because of Polkadot's interoperability, it has become effortless to transfer assets between different blockchains, and Polkadot has the highest potential transaction speeds currently in the industry. DOT cannot be staked, but it can be invested in through Bitvavo for crypto 2022.

What makes Polkadot a good investment?

Polkadot can communicate with other networks, including Ethereum. Polkadot has a growing number of programmers, in a webinar Keith Bliss (President Capital2Markets) discussed this, "Polkadot is an Ethereum competitor and many programmers use it because it is more secure. It allows them to build their own blockchains."

Polkadot addresses scalability, a major blockchain problem. Polkadot's parachains reduce congestion. This enhanced feature also makes it a good investment choice.

Vitalik Buterin, one of Polkadot's founders, also co-founded Ethereum, giving it a strong foundation and support from many investors.

Cosmos [ATOM] 2022

Cosmos considers itself a project that solves some of the "most difficult problems" facing the blockchain industry. It is intended to provide an antidote to "slow, expensive, non-scalable and environmentally damaging" proof-of-work protocols, such as those currently used by Bitcoin.

The project's other goals include making blockchain technology less complex and difficult for developers thanks to a modular framework that demystifies decentralized apps. Last but not least, an Inter

Blockchain communication protocol makes it easier for blockchain networks to communicate with each other, preventing fragmentation in the industry. ATOM cannot be staked, but it can be invested in through Bitvavo.

What makes Cosmos a good investment?

Staking is an additional income generator with ATOM coins for investors who want to hold ATOM and earn an additional return. At Binance, you can strike ATOM and other cryptocoins.

Cosmos is described as "Blockchain 3.0" - has big goal to make sure the infrastructure is easy to use. This allows a network to be easily built using pieces of code that already exist. In the long run, it is hoped that this will make complex applications easy to produce.

Scalability is another priority, meaning that significantly more transactions can be processed per second than more old-fashioned blockchains like Bitcoin and Ethereum.

Polygon [MATIC] 2022
Polygon (formerly Matic Network) is the first well-structured, easy-to-use platform for Ethereum scaling and infrastructure development. Its core component is Polygon SDK, a modular, flexible framework that supports building multiple types of applications. Polygon effectively transforms Ethereum into a full-fledged multi-chain system (also known as Internet of Blockchains). This multi-chain system is akin to other

systems such as Polkadot, Cosmos, Avalanche, etc. With the advantages of Ethereum's security, vibrant ecosystem and openness. MATIC cannot be staked, but can be invested in through Bitvavo.

What makes Polygon a good investment?
You can think of Polygon crypto as an express train. It is on the same track as all other trains, but runs faster and makes fewer stops along the way. In this example, the track is Ethereum, where Polygon conducts transactions faster than other crypto networks.
The platform uses a POS or proof-of-stake consensus to secure the network and create a new currency.
Polygon boasts up to 65,000 transactions per second on a single side chain, along with a respectable transaction time of less than two seconds.

Algorand [ALGO] 2022

Algorand is one of the most popular open-source platforms using blockchain technology. Algorand as a decentralized network is intentionally built to solve the three pressing problems of blockchain technology, namely decentralization, speed and security.

Algorand is used to create applications for digital assets, identity, securities, logistics chains, infrastructure, stablecoins, environment, government/public sector, financial institutions, decentralized finance (DeFi), gaming and insurance.

What makes Algorand a good investment?

One of the applications built for identity FLEXFINTX has been invaluable in helping over 400 million Africans obtain a digital identity.

Algorand is designed to have lower transaction costs, as well as no use of mining (like Bitcoin's energy-intensive process), because it is based on the proof-of-stake (PoS) blockchain protocol.

Investors can buy the Algorand coin ALGO through crypto exchanges like Bitvavo, and it is considered one of the best crypto coins 2022.

Enjin [ENJ] 2022

Enjin Coin is a blockchain cryptocurrency uniquely aimed at gamers. In 2017, the Singapore-based Enjin company launched this currency as an ERC-20 compliant token. What that means is that you can send and receive ENJ using an Ethereum wallet. Much more interesting, however, is what ENJ is spent on. Most cryptocurrencies are usable to buy something.
ENJ has a unique usability that is part of how the coin works. Gamers can use ENJ to buy NFTs in various games. NFTs or non-replaceable tokens are used to buy digital content only and are currently very popular which you can see in the current price at Bitvavo.

What makes Enjin a good investment?
Enjin Coin uses a series of smart contracts that game developers send ENJ to create new, unique replaceable or non-replaceable ERC-1155 tokens. These tokens can

be traded on the Enjin Marketplace or redeemed for their backing ENJ. As more custom tokens are minted, more ENJ is removed from the ecosystem, making it more scarce.

Enjin co-founder Witek Radomski wrote the code for one of the very first non-fungible tokens (NFTs) and is also the co-author of the ERC-1155 Ethereum token standard.

With the growing success of NFTs, Enjin is likely to experience a high price appreciation and is also seen as one of the best altcoins 2022.

Long term profit strategies

Cryptocurrencies have had a difficult start to the year amid multiple concerns in the industry. The biggest concern is the Federal Reserve, which has pledged to act more aggressively in its fight against inflation. Coins have also crashed because of rising fears about valuations in the cryptocurrency industry.

Cryptocurrencies such as Bitcoin, Ethereum, Ripple and Cardano have all fallen by more than 50% from their highest point ever. In this article, we will highlight the ten best cryptocurrencies to invest in for long-term gains.

Bitcoin
Bitcoin is a leading cryptocurrency started in 2009 by Satoshi Nakamoto. The currency was created as an alternative to fiat currencies such as the U.S. dollar and the euro. The difference is that it would be decentralized in nature, meaning that no single entity would have much power over it.

At its peak, Bitcoin was trading at nearly $70,000. Now it has crashed to around $25,000 as concerns about the Federal Reserve increase. Still, there is a chance that the price of the currency will do well in the future. Unlike other currencies, it is significantly safe and supply is dropping significantly.

Furthermore, Bitcoin has been embraced by some of the largest entities in the world. For example, Tesla owns Bitcoin worth more than $1 billion. Similarly, companies such as MicroStrategy and Square have Bitcoin on their balance sheets. Therefore, the price of Bitcoin is likely to be a good long-term investment.

Ether

Ether is the original token for the Ethereum ecosystem. Ethereum is a leading blockchain that enables developers to build high-quality decentralized applications across all industries. It is possible for people to build apps in areas such as decentralized finance (DeFi), non-replaceable tokens (NFT) and metaverse.

Ethereum has become a major player in these industries. For example, it was used to build apps like Axie Infinity, Aave, Curve Finance and Decentraland. As the blockchain industry is expected to continue to grow, Ethereum is likely to continue to play an important role.

Ethereum is also a good investment because of its move from a proof-of-work to a proof-of-stake network. This move, combined with the embrace of sharding technology, will lead to more demand. Therefore, there is a possibility that the price of Ethereum will continue to do well.

ATOOM

ATOM is the native token for the Cosmos ecosystem. Cosmos is a leading blockchain platform that helps connect multiple coins. According to its website, it has hundreds of tokens with a total value of billions. At the same time, its SDK is used to build some of the industry's leading blockchain platforms, such as ThorChain and Osmosis. The price of ATOM will do well as the growth of the ecosystem continues.

The Sandbox

The Sandbox is one of the largest metaverse industry. It is a platform that allows people and businesses to buy virtual real estate online. It has also become one of the leading platforms for trading virtual non-fungible tokens (NFT). Furthermore, it is a leading gaming ecosystem that allows people to play virtual games in tournaments known as Alpha. The token SAND is likely to continue to rise in the long run.

MKR

MKR is the native token for the Maker ecosystem. Maker is a leading DeFi platform that allows people to borrow and save in the network. It differs from other DeFi platforms simply because of its own stablecoin known as Dai. Furthermore, unlike other platforms, it uses its own oracle system. Thus, there is a chance that the MKR price will rise in the long run, especially after the collapse of Anchor Protocol.

LINK

LINK is another popular cryptocurrency that is a good long-term investment. It is a leading platform that allows blockchain developers to simplify their development process. It does so by helping them incorporate off-chain data into the on-chain.

It has the largest market share in the industry and is used by leading DeFi platforms such as Aave and Uniswap. With its market share and strong growth, there is a chance that it will do well in the long run.

Will bitcoin hit the 100k in 2022?

The Bitcoin price forecast for 2021 turned out to be a little different for many investors. But despite high expectations, Bitcoin still performed well. With a return of 64% in 2021, Bitcoin left all other investment assets far behind. Many analysts, as well as many retail investors, had expected the Bitcoin price to reach $100,000 by the end of 2021.

In reality, crypto prices, including Bitcoin's, lagged a bit behind in this regard. What does this have to do with and will Bitcoin still get to 100K in 2022?

Crypto prices are difficult to predict, but we would like to know if investing in Bitcoin is still wise and if 100K is a possibility. To give you a hand with this, you can look at a number of events and changes. Once upon a time, of course, Bitcoin was also conceived for a reason. The impetus was the financial crisis in 2008 and now so many years later, the financial system appears to be in even worse shape.

Someone who doesn't believe in Bitcoin probably won't invest either. But if you are interested, maybe after reading this article, you will look at it differently. What I mention are facts, plus my own opinion. Both have come about by doing my own research. Therefore, this article is absolutely not intended as investment advice. With the information I only try to show you if and how important Bitcoin could become in the future.

Sand in the engine
As of January 1, 2021, the Bitcoin price doubled from
$25,500 to $51,000 within three months. Not only
Bitcoin did well, by the way, other crypto prices such as
Ethereum also did well. There was a lot of talk about it
and it rained predictions. The Bitcoin price expectation
for 2021 was for many - reaching the magic limit of
$100,000. One of those predictors was Plan B.

Plan B is known for its Stock-to-Flow model (S2F). That
model thus predicted $100,000 by the end of 2021 and,
with an improved model, even a Bitcoin price of
$288,000 by 2024. Although Plan B is a well-known
Dutchman, he remains anonymous in the media. With
his model, he measures the scarcity of Bitcoin, so to
speak. This is done by dividing the current supply (stock)
of Bitcoin by the number of Bitcoins produced annually
(flow).

And because the reward for mining halves on average
every four years, Bitcoins come to the market at an
increasingly slow pace. If demand for the currency
continues to grow, a Bitcoin price expectation of 100K is
quite possible in the short term. Especially since the
number of Bitcoins is set at a maximum of 21 million.

By the way, the Plan B model dates back to March 2019
and lasted until early December 2021. For many, it was
a shock that the prediction suddenly stopped being
true. Will Bitcoin still go to 100K in 2022? Yes, according
to Plan B it will, he says he is still confident. The model

is still intact in his eyes. Although we should start seeing signs of recovery in the first few months of 2022.

Too much guided by predictions
Of course, his Bitcoin price prediction is not wrong, which is why it is understandable that people are watching his model closely. It seemed only a matter of patience before Bitcoin would reach 100K.

Of course, it happens regularly that predictions are made, both positive and negative. Only you have so little use for them.

Still, his model, based on scarcity, looks quite credible. Only what does it do to your emotions, when the Bitcoin price no longer follows the model?

In reality, it was even worse; Bitcoin did not even make it to $50,000. All in all, a big disappointment that turned into fear.

After the last peak (for now) on November 9, 2021, the Bitcoin price is currently $18,000 in the minus. News about the Omikron variant, as well as high inflation and the current crisis, seemed to be the cause of the price drop. And what about China, which strictly bans cryptocurrency. When uncertainty reigns, you often see money being pulled out of risky investments first.

Cryptocurrency, of course, is one of them. On the other hand, when money is worth less, people look for ways to protect themselves against it.

More uncertainty
Besides the fact that inflation is high, it is precisely the
low interest rates that are worrying. Normally the ECB
(European Bank) can influence inflation by playing with
interest rates. The only thing they can do now is throw
the interest rate up, lower is no longer possible.

But in a crisis they prefer not to throw the interest rate
up. The moment the interest rate goes up, borrowing
becomes more expensive and less money will be spent.
And the lowering of interest rates plus the billions in
stimulus packages are precisely meant to keep the
economy going.

The high inflation is probably not temporary either and
there is a risk that it will rise even further. This means
that fiat money is worth less and less and as long as
saving is not interesting, people will continue to look for
alternatives.

Bright spots
The amount of money that has been printed recently is,
of course, one of the reasons for inflation. According to
economist Edin Mujagic, the past shows that printing
money on a large scale has never ended well. He does
not see why it will end well this time. Edin grew up in
Yugoslavia and argues that the war back then was
ultimately caused by hyperinflation. What particularly
worries him are the similarities he sees with the former
Yugoslavia and the financial situation in the Netherlands
and Europe now.

This can certainly not be called a bright spot and it is certain that the bill will have to be paid one day. What exactly that will mean for us I dare not say. But it is good to think about this. It is not for nothing that 2021 was the year when many institutional investors decided to also start investing in Bitcoin and other cryptocurrencies.

Even countries like El Salvador and the Ukraine are stockpiling Bitcoins. Of course, institutional parties and countries would not invest in Bitcoin if they did not believe in it. The main reason people invest is because Bitcoin is scarce and they want to protect themselves from inflation. It is not crazy to think that the growing interest and acceptance of Bitcoin will continue to increase in the coming decades. Maybe 100K for 2022 is just a bit too ambitious, but that this limit will be reached I am convinced.

Want to better understand how our current money system was created and works (or rather no longer works).

Post covid economy

Two years of corona has had a clear impact on the way people spend their money. Although total credit card spending is almost back to 2019 levels - with a -2% decrease - the distribution of spending has totally changed. In particular, there has been a large increase in purchases of second-hand items. With a growth of +144%, this is the fastest growing product category.

The category that has grown the fastest in terms of credit card spending is the financial services category. This is due to purchases of crypto coins which increased by +1,580%.

However, spending on travel and restaurants has not yet returned to its previous level. This is according to ICS Credit Card Facts, an analysis by ICS of credit card data in the period Q1 2019 - Q1 2022.

The shifts in the data give a good picture of the changed choices consumers made in recent years. Second-hand items are doing remarkably well. People had more time to make major changes to their homes and put unnecessary items up for sale due to the lockdowns. Crypto currencies were also bought in abundance over the past two years.

People had money left over that they would otherwise have spent on vacations or hospitality and had more time to learn the ins & outs around trading crypto. A third notable riser, the "digital services" category, grew by 41%. This was mainly due to an increase in spending on streaming services.

Categories that are still recovering

There are also categories that have traditionally performed well, but have not yet returned to their former levels. For example, we see that the category 'Food & Beverage' is still performing 17% lower compared to two years ago. This is mainly due to a decline in spending at restaurants, as we were still in lockdown for much of January. Spending there is in Q1 2022, 27% lower than the same period in 2019. Spending on food delivery did rise sharply by 355%. In travel, we see the same picture with a decrease of 11%. However, recent credit card spending does show the recovery of the travel sector. Spending in Q1 of this year is +312% higher than in Q1 2021. Entertainment is down -9%, mainly due to -13% spending on film & theater.

Lots of credit card spending in Austria and Iceland

Trends in credit card spending in 50 countries worldwide were examined. The biggest riser in hotel spending in Q1 2022 compared to the same quarter a year earlier is Austria with +4.260%. At number two is Iceland with +2380% and at third place Norway with +1279%. It should be obvious that the growth in spending at Austrian hotels is due to tourists who were able to return to the Austrian ski slopes and après-ski this year. The growing spending at the tollbooths is undoubtedly also related to the increase in winter sports enthusiasts. With travel restrictions in place to

countries outside Europe, "special" destinations within
Europe - such as Iceland and Norway - may have gained
popularity.

Fraud increased

With the advent of corona and the rapid rise of online
shopping, the proportion of rogue webshops also
increased. Glenn Mac Donald, CCO of ICS: "We have had
turbulent years and this is clearly reflected in our data
on fraud. ICS continuously monitors whether sites are
potentially fraudulent and acts quickly. That is why we
took about 350 websites offline in the past quarter and
preventively replaced almost 5,000 cards. When paying
with a credit card, the purchase protection and
insurance usually ensures that consumers get their
money back even in the event of fraud." He continues:
"We also see very clearly in our data that the digital
transition has accelerated tremendously. People often
had to make their purchases online due to the
lockdowns and they continued to do so. As a result,
compared to 2019, purchases online increased by 34%,
but offline spending decreased by 23%. In subsequent
Credit Card Facts analyses, we're going to see to what
extent offline purchases are still going to recover or
whether the digital transition is proving to be
permanent in certain categories."

How should you start with cryptocurrency investments?

A prerequisite to success is achieving a goal. Don't start cryptocurrency as a headless chicken. Start with a goal. Why do you want to start with cryptocurrency? What is your investment goal? From experience, I would like to give you the tip to always think long term.

For example, set a concrete goal: within [xx years], I want to have x amount of money in assets thanks to investing.

This is an all-encompassing goal to investing. Starting to invest in crypto currencies should be a part of this. Successful investors spread her opportunities. Understand that crypto currencies are extremely risky. You don't want to put all your money on one horse. Not even if this is a very fast horse (with fragile ankles). Because this is how investing in crypto works
Dear long term investor, here you can read all about investing in crypto. From investing in crypto for beginners to the best crypto apps. Including extensive tutorial (explanation) on how online investing in.
: it can rise fast, but also fall hard.

If I may give you a tip/guideline, it is to not put more than 10% of your total investment assets in crypto.

This may not be what you want to read. But I want to protect you from big money losses. Especially as a novice investor, you can go huge on your luck with

95

cryptocurrency. The purpose of this article is to teach you how to successfully start investing in crypto currencies. Not how to get rich quick or poor quick....

Successful investors spread opportunities to achieve the investment goal. Invest in other assets besides crypto. I'll come back to this later ☺ .

So within your overall goal, you need to know how crypto investing is going to contribute to it.

Start investing in crypto currencies yourself or outsource the process?

Starting with cryptocurrency is risky. Nevertheless, it can be lucrative to invest a small portion in it. After all, high risk can also lead to potentially high returns.

The question is: how do you want to start crypto investing? Basically, you have two options: you start investing yourself, or you let others do it.

In general, with your own efforts, you can potentially get higher returns. This is only true if you have the right knowledge and skills. And since starting with crypto is quite risky, it may not be unwise to have it outsourced. This gives a number of advantages, such as that you don't need any time or knowledge for it. A disadvantage is that it comes with a cost. The question is whether you will perform better at the bottom line (return - cost) if you do it yourself.

If you want to get started with cryptocurrency and would rather outsource it (which, frankly, may be wise).

Start with diversification and research: put together a crypto investment portfolio

Successful investors don't just choose diversification. They also do a lot of research on the best investments. Particularly with individual stocks and crypto coins, your success hinges on research. You only want to invest in the best crypto coins, right? With stocks, this is easier: you can analyze companies for future growth (in profits). With crypto coins, this is not possible. However, you can look at future potential.

You guessed it: future potential also means that this potential may not be achieved. It is more uncertain than with stocks. Shares are of physical companies that make profits (or losses). Crypto currencies are (for now) mostly ideas or concepts. This is why starting with cryptocurrency is so risky.

The solution? Put together a crypto investment portfolio. In the context of risk diversification, such a portfolio should consist of at least the top 15 most popular crypto coins. And ideally the top 30.

Start with diversification and research: build a crypto investment portfolio

Successful investors don't just choose diversification. They also do a lot of research on the best investments.

Particularly with individual stocks and crypto coins, your success hinges on research. You only want to invest in the best crypto coins, right? With stocks, this is easier: you can analyze companies for future growth (in profits). With crypto coins, this is not possible. However, you can look at future potential.

You guessed it: future potential also means that this potential may not be achieved. It is more uncertain than with stocks. Shares are of physical companies that make profits (or losses). Crypto currencies are (for now) mostly ideas or concepts. This is why starting with cryptocurrency is so risky.

The solution? Put together a crypto investment portfolio. In the context of risk diversification, such a portfolio should consist of at least the top 15 most popular crypto coins. And ideally the top 30.

Sure enough, diversification decreases the potential return. Suppose you invest $1000 in the best crypto currency. You might then achieve a return of +500% (that's x6). But for the same thing it goes wrong and you lose all your money.

Isn't it better to spread $1000 over 30 crypto coins? Then you might get a lower return of, say, +100% (in the long run). But the downside potential is also lower. After all, if 1 of the 30 coins performs excellently with x30 return, this gives $33.3 x 30 = $999 return.

The probability of positive returns increases with diversification through a crypto portfolio.

Do you want to start successfully with cryptocurrency investing? Our tip is to choose a crypto portfolio. Increase your chance of profit and decrease your chance of losing money.

Start with a small, monthly deposit

Want to make high returns with cryptocurrency? The best way is buy low, sell high. This means active crypto trading where you sell at peaks and buy in declines. The chart above shows how to go about this.

On a graph it looks easy. So why do so many crypto investors lose money? Because we are emotional creatures. The crypto market is exciting and volatile. Everyone is waiting for the next hype. And once that happens, it seems like the sky is the limit. On a day-to-day level, it's hard to act rationally.

Tip: Want to sell high and buy low? Turn off your emotions and work with automatic limit orders. Take a step back and look at the market on a "monthly level", rather than a "daily level".

This takes knowledge and skill. This is not suitable for starting out with cryptocurrency. There may be a better strategy for beginners.

As a beginner, you may achieve more success with the following strategy:

Invest only with money you can spare
Invest a small amount every month in your crypto portfolio.

Do this for multiple consecutive years (if you believe in cryptocurrency)

Buy extra when the crypto market drops sharply (e.g. -30% or even -70%).

Sell part of your deposit at large spikes (e.g. at +50% or +100%). Set this amount aside and bet according to step 2 and/or step 4.
Or cash the profit and put it in your savings account or lower-risk investments.

Of course it is better to buy only in the big crashes. But there are many (emotional) factors that lead you to make mistakes in market timing. With a monthly deposit you aim for an average purchase price of the market. If the market rises in the long run, you will make returns.

What you should never do is only buy at hype and spikes!

Did you know that investing just 100 dollars a month in crypto can lead to $373,960 in wealth over 30 years?

Work on your knowledge and skills for successful crypto investing

You've created an account and put together a crypto portfolio. You start with a monthly deposit. In case of a big market crash, you buy a little extra. Great: this is a successful start to investing in cryptocurrency. How to proceed?

Knowledge is power.

Successful investors invest in assets that they know will yield profits in the future. Investing has risks. So knowing is never 100% certainty, but rather a high probability of approaching 100%.

The next step in successfully starting with cryptocurrency is by working on your knowledge and skills. Get to know the market. Gain experience. Research potential crypto coins. A helpful website for this is coinmarketcap.com. And so you can find a lot of information on the Internet. You can also network and visit crypto events.

Who knows, you might become very experienced. Who knows, maybe you'll soon be able to track down potentially useful crypto coins. The more advanced you become, the higher your chances of winning.

A useful skill in cryptocurrency is learning day trading.

With stocks and ETFs, I prefer buy & hold. This means holding for the long term. In crypto, they call this HODL. I think HODL works with the most popular and potential crypto currencies. But with the smaller crypto, this is probably not the case because much of it is "hot air". Short-term buying and selling may work better with cryptocurrency.

Experienced day traders can make a lot of money
Make more money? Many roads lead to Rome, but only a handful of ideas are the best way to make extra money. Make money quickly and easily from home, or from employment. It is possible. I...
 With crypto currencies. This is because the crypto market is very volatile. On a daily level, there are large peaks and valleys (e.g. 10%). I am not a day trader myself. In fact, I have an aversion to it. But that doesn't mean it might be for you.

Become a successful investor

You now know how to get started with cryptocurrency. Probably in a successful way. Are you ready to take it a step further? Do you want to become a successful investor?

Do you want sustainable financial success?

Then set up a diversified long-term investment portfolio. This can consist of various investments in (not limited to):

- Exchange Traded Funds (ETFs) and/or mutual funds
- Real estate and property funds
- Loans like bonds, crowdfunding and P2P Lending

(Dividend) equities
There are (too?) many opportunities to get started. Perhaps you can start with lower-risk investments in addition to crypto. You can read examples in this article about how to invest with fixed returns. These kinds of investments give you more stability

How much should you invest monthly in Crypto and Bitcoin to earn profit?

These days, investing in cryptos yourself is simple. There are now reliable parties with acceptable transaction costs. They also allow you to create a free account and easily transfer money in and out with crypto and credit cards. Think of crypto platforms such as Coinbase, Binance and Bitfinex.

However, it is a completely different story to get the best results with investing in crypto yourself. This requires knowledge, time and a good investment strategy. Many people who invest in cryptos themselves lose money. It is better to choose a middle ground here, such as a crypto portfolio or having experts invest. Remember well that anyone can invest when the market is rising. What do you do when your money evaporates by -50%?

Risk and return when investing in crypto and bitcoin on a monthly basis
Investing has great risks. Money loss is a regular occurrence. To be successful, risk diversification is an absolute must. Long-term investing and doing a lot of research is also necessary.

On the question of how much monthly investing in crypto and Bitcoin, we must consider the risk and return

In the stock market, we talk about an average annual return of 8 - 10% per year. This is over a long term of 20 - 30 years. One year may be +30%. The other year -20%. As with crypto and Bitcoin, you can also invest more riskily with stocks. The best investors in the world thus achieve an average annual return of >25%.

With crypto and Bitcoin, it is, for me, uncertain what an average annual return could be. The market is still too young for that. With Bitcoin, one year is -80%, and the next year is +500%. The volatility is extreme. And that creates opportunities.

To give a sensible answer to how much we want to invest in crypto coins each month, we have to make assumptions. Below you can read which ones they are. Then we're going to see concrete calculations as an answer to our question.

Assumption of average annual returns in Bitcoin and crypto

To determine how much to invest monthly in crypto and Bitcoin, we have to make assumptions. I'm an optimist, even though I don't believe in Bitcoin all that much (but I do believe in the blockchain

In the long term 20 to 30 years, the demand for crypto and Bitcoin will increase.
The assumption is 15% average return per year with a diversified crypto portfolio (at least the top 30 largest coins)

This is achievable with active investing: buy the dip, and sell frequently at peaks.
An average of 15% per year is high. I do think this is realistic with more active investing. In doing so, you do need to build a crypto portfolio.

In the long term 20 to 30 years, the demand for crypto and Bitcoin will increase.

The assumption is 15% average return per year with a diversified crypto portfolio (at least the top 30 largest coins)
This is achievable with active investing: buy the dip, and sell frequently at peaks.

An average of 15% per year is high. I do think this is realistic with more active investing. In doing so, you do need to build a crypto portfolio.

With Bitcoin and crypto currencies, these peaks and valleys are much more extreme. And that's why I think 15% is realistic for an advanced crypto investor.

Important starting point is that you don't take too much risk. Personally, I think of max 10% of your total assets monthly invested in crypto and Bitcoin. More or less is also possible. It is completely your risk and realize that you can lose a lot of money.

Finally, crypto and Bitcoin are not (yet) a passive investment. Take advantage of the price volatility. You do this by selling high and buying low. Use limit orders for automation and avoidance of emotional decisions.

Now comes the fun part: how much monthly investing in crypto and Bitcoin for 100K to even 1 million?

How much should you be investing each month into crypto and Bitcoin for 100,000 dollars?

Scenario thinking is necessary when facing an uncertain future. Monthly investing in crypto and Bitcoin is extremely uncertain. Our starting point is 15% average return per year. This is an assumption. But you believe in crypto and Bitcoin, and so you decide to invest in them monthly. You take the risk for granted. You invest only with money that you can miss 100%.

Let's look at three scenarios:

Worst-case scenario: -10% average return p.a. over 20 years
Most-likely scenario: 15% average annual return over 20 years
Best-case scenario: 20% average return p.a. over 20 years
In this article we continue to use these scenarios. Worst-case is not included, although it is a realistic scenario. As most-likely, we take our assumption of 15%.

Given the uncertainty, it is necessary to use an active investment strategy where you mainly "buy the dip" (buy low). And ideally sell high from time to time to convert some of your profits to cash for the next dip.

How much monthly investment in crypto and Bitcoin for 100,000 dollars in 20 years?

Answer: 100 - 150 dollars per month.

With a small amount of money, you could build a large fortune. This is because the return stands at 15%, which is seriously high. We are being optimistic here. Too optimistic? Time will tell. (Although 15% is considerably lower than the last five years).

But still. Even with stocks, you can build a large fortune with a small amount of money. That's the power of long-term returns.

How much should you be investing each month into crypto and Bitcoin for 250,000 dollars?

Let's be more ambitious and aim for a bigger amount. How much monthly investment in crypto and Bitcoin for 250,000 dollars in 20 years?

Answer: 300 - 350 dollars per month

Note that with a higher deposit you will probably exceed the 10%. Suppose you want to invest $500 monthly. At max 10% investing in crypto, that's "only" $50 per month. Again, personally I would not go higher than 10%. Understand well that it comes with huge risks.

How much should you be investing each month into crypto and Bitcoin for 1 million dollars?
Let's look at one more scenario to unlearn. How much monthly investing in crypto and Bitcoin for 1 million euros? This sounds like a staggering amount of money. However, the truth is that anyone can make it. Even with 8% returns!

There are two conditions though. Long-term investing is the first. Becoming a millionaire in 20 years is feasible but difficult. In 30 years is easier (see chart below). Secondly, you will have to put in a lot of money every month. You should only do this if you can miss it 100%. It can also go wrong.

If I can do it, you can do it too. (Especially since I am not a super investor)

So: how much monthly investing in crypto and bitcoin for 1 million euros within 20 years?

Answer: 1300 - 1500 dollars per month

Important: at 10% return and monthly $1000 deposit you will also have 1 million after 30 years. 10% return is more realistic than 15%. This is achievable with a diversified investment portfolio in stocks, ETFs, real estate and alternatives. This significantly reduces the risk. In other words, the security to 1 million increases!